How th
Can Hear

Written by Kate Scott

Collins

Ears are terrific.

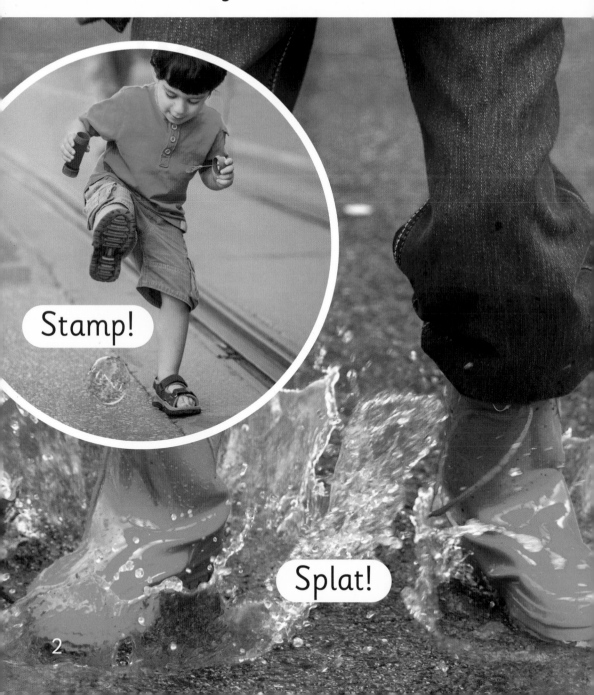

Stamp!

Splat!

They help us to hear.

Scrunch!

Crack!

Ears keep you alert.

You can still hear if you rest or nap.

This is what the parts of an ear look like.

ear

ear canal

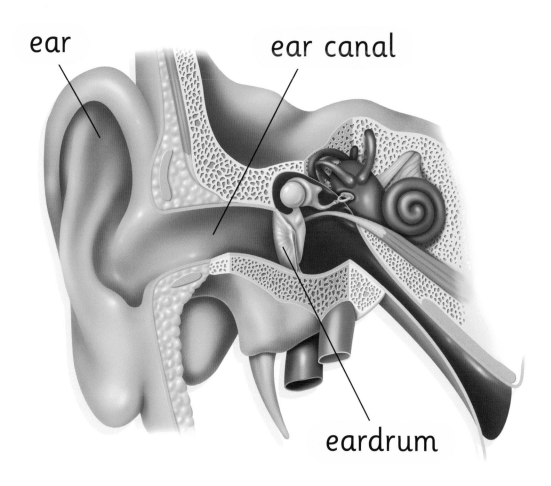

eardrum

Do not stick objects in ears.
You might hurt them!

The little hairs deep in ears help us to hear.

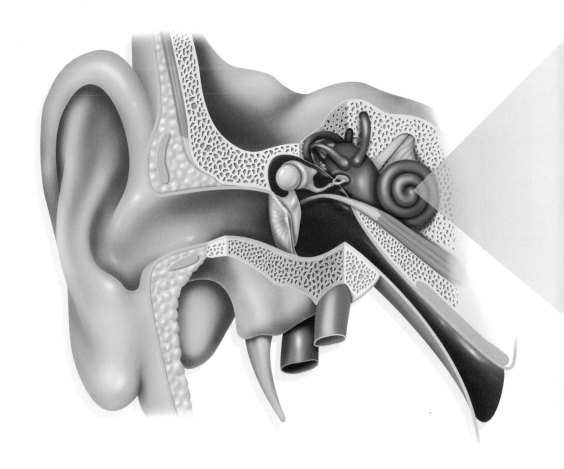

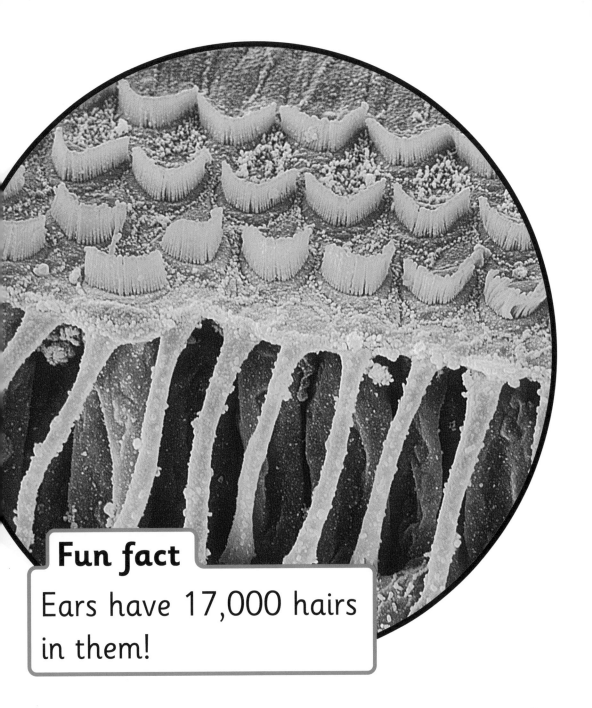

Fun fact

Ears have 17,000 hairs in them!

Wax keeps dust out of ears.

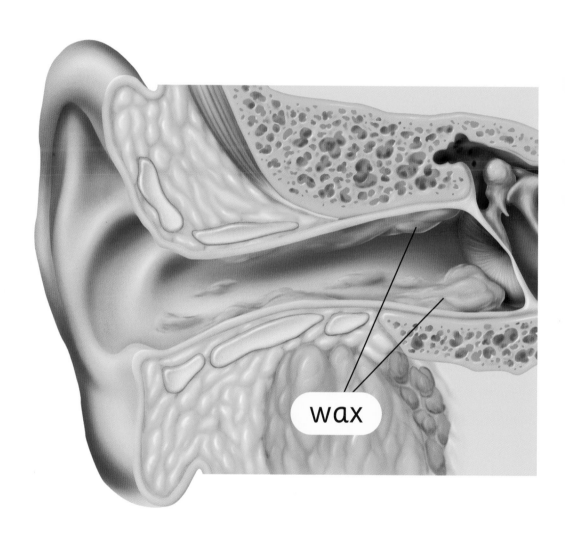

wax

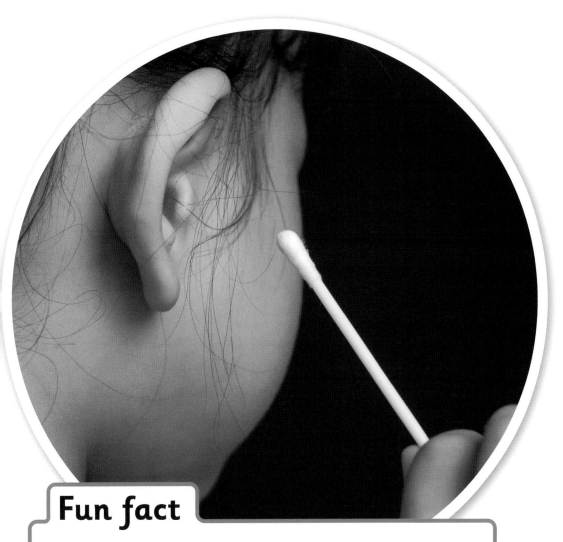

Fun fact

Do not stick cotton buds in ears.
The wax will come out by itself.

Lots of things can help if you cannot hear well.

13

In the ear

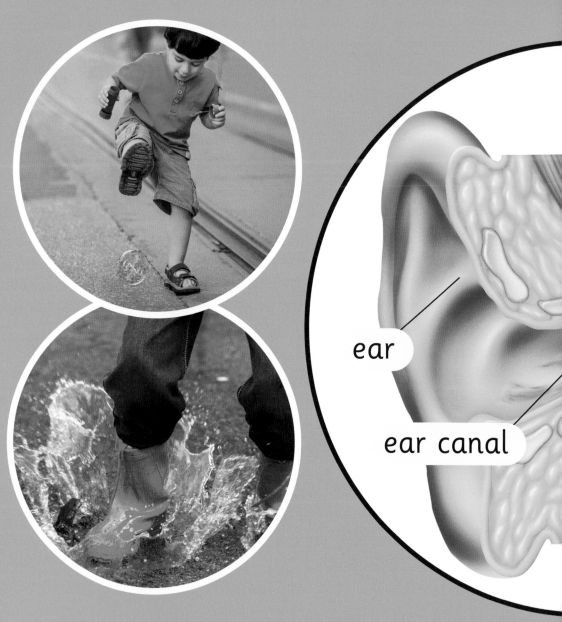

ear

ear canal

wax

eardrum

Review: After reading

Use your assessment from hearing the children read to choose any GPCs, words or tricky words that need additional practice.

Read 1: Decoding

- Practise reading words that contain adjacent consonants. Model sounding out the following word, saying each of the sounds quickly and clearly. Then blend the sounds together.

  f/a/c/t   fact

- Ask the children to say each of the sounds in the following words. Now ask them to blend the sounds together.

  stamp   scrunch   splat

- Now ask the children if they can read each of the words without sounding them out.

Read 2: Prosody

- Model reading each page with expression to the children.
- After you have read each page, ask the children to have a go at reading with expression, drawing their attention to sentences with exclamation marks for emphasis.

Read 3: Comprehension

- For every question ask the children how they know the answer.
  - Look at page 6 together. Talk about the labels and ask the children why they are used. (*to tell us the names of things in the diagram*)
  - Turn to pages 14 and 15. Using the images for support, ask the children what they learnt about ears and hearing from the book.